Ultimate Buye
Porsche Carrera, Tu
Conten

GW00599299

Porsche 911 Carrera, Turbo & GT (996)

Introduction

This Ultimate Buyers' Guide helps you identify and buy the Porsche 911 Carrera, Turbo or GT models, manufactured between 1997 and 2005 and known widely by its internal type number, 996.

The guide includes facts and figures, year by year changes, special models and information on colours and the generally-available (non-motorsport) options available for all the models.

The buying section tells you what to look for when viewing a 996 and gives invaluable tips on how to select the most desirable models and options.

The 911 range is unique in offering a sports car design concept that has been honed and developed over 40 years.

The 996 is the latest model to reflect the 911 series rich history of motor sport success combined with almost universal praise for its superb dynamics, performance, reliability and residual values.

The 996 has emerged as the best selling 911 variant of all time and this is not without reason. Porsche were very shrewd in developing the latest model with more of mainstream appeal, treading a fine line between retaining the car's timeless appeal and aiming to attract buyers away from the other prestige sports saloon manufacturers.

The sleek new bodyshell and more functional modern interior, combined with greatly improved ride comfort, made the new 911 easier to live with than the earlier models.

But there has been no softening of Porsche's resolve to keep the 911 at the top of international motorsport and enthusiasts' ownership aspirations. There are plenty of special models and the options list includes everything from sports suspension and exhausts, to special bodykits. The GT3 and GT2 models are as extreme as any driver could wish.

The roadgoing versions have lost none of their driving charisma either. With 300bhp (221kW), improved handling and brakes and that lighter and more slippery bodyshell, the Carrera is seriously fast and still a great drivers' machine.

For impartial advice on suitable service centres, the best places to buy spare parts and other useful contacts, you should join your national Porsche club.

This guide aims to give you all the core information you need to select and buy a 996. If you are unfamiliar with the risks of buying a used model, then for increased peace of mind, have any potential purchase properly inspected by a Porsche-only specialist.

Grant Neal and Peter Morgan
England

Timeline for the 996

This timeline (and the references used throughout the text) is divided into the automobile industry model years. For instance, this would define a 1999 model as being produced between 1st Augu 1998 and 31st July 1999.

1997
In autumn 1997 the new 911 Carrerra (Type 996) was introduced with 300bhp (221kW) wat cooled flat-6 engine. Carrera 2 (rear-wheel drive) and in coupé bodystyle only.

1999
Improved specification models with POSIP (Porsche Side Impact Protection System), bet exhaust sound and clear turn signal lenses. Carrera 4 with Porsche Stability Management (PSN Cabriolet and GT3 (360bhp, 265kW) introduced.

2000
Upgrades include E-gas throttle (drive by wire), upgraded engine management and Porsc Stability Management (PSM) available as an option on Carrera 2. New 420bhp (309kW) Turbo a 'Millennium' limited edition Carrera introduced.

2001
Further detail improvements including front compartment and engine cover electronic release w new switches both inside the car and by a remote control key fob. February 2001, presentation of t 462bhp (340kW) GT2 (with ceramic brakes).

2002
Major upgrade with enlarged 320bhp (235kW) 3.6-litre engine with Variocam Plus technology a more aggressive sound. 'Facelift' with teardrop style front headlamps and restyled bumpers front a rear. Improved aerodynamics, rigidity and crash protection. Upgraded interior quality and improv spec. to include On Board Computer (OBC), three spoke steering wheel, glovebox and cuphold Cabriolet gets glass rear window. New Targa and Carrera 4S (with Turbo widebody) launched.

2003
New facelift, uprated GT3 introduced.

2004
C4S and Turbo Cabriolets launched ,GT3 RS introduced with 381bhp (284kW). '40 years of 911' anniversary special edition Carrera (345bhp, 235kW).GT2 uprated. New Turbo S unveiled w 450bhp and ceramic brakes as standard. At year end 996 (except C4S, Turbo S) replaced by 997

2001 911 GT2

Facts, figures and performance

Containing Porsche's official data, this gives you a direct comparison between all th
models without the variables introduced by various magazine tests, with different cars, dr
conditions. This section includes summary information on engine capacity/ power & to
weight/ bhp & torque to weight (an excellent guide to real world performance comparis

	C2	C2Cab	C4	C4Cab
Engine capacity	3397cc F-3596cc	3397cc F-3596cc	3397cc F-3596cc	3397cc F-3596cc
Maximum power & Maximum torque	221/235kW (300/320bhp) at 6800 rpm 350/370Nm (258/273lbft) at 4600/4250rpm	221/235kW (300/320bhp) at 6800rpm 350/370Nm (258/273lbft) at 4600/4250rpm	221/235kW (300/320bhp) at 6800 rpm 350/370Nm (258/273lbft) at 4600/4250rpm	221/235kW (300/320bhp) a 6800rpm 350/3 (258/273lbft) ai 4600/4250rpm
Weight (DIN)/Kg	man/tip 1320/1365kg 1345/1400kg	man/tip 1395/1440kg 1425/1480kg	man/tip 1375/1420kg 1405/1460kg	man/tip 1450/1495kg 1485/1540kg
Power/ Torque per Tonne (showing Manual & Tiptronic)	M-227bhp/195lbft 238bhp/203lbft T- 220bhp/189lb ft 228bhp/195lbft	M-215bhp/185lbft 224bhp/192lbft T- 208bhp/179lbft 216bhp/184lbft	M-218bhp/188lbft 228bhp/194lbft T- 211bhp/182lbft 219bhp/187lbft	M-207bhp/178 215bhp/184 T- 201bhp/172 208bhp/177
0-62 & 0-99mph (0-100/160km/h)	Man-5.2/ 11.5 5/ 11 Tip- 6/ 13 5.5/ 12	5.4/ 11.9 5.2/ 11.4 6.2/ 13.4 5.7/ 12.4	5.2/ 11.6 5/ 11.1 6 /13.1 5.5/ 12.1	5.4/ 12 5.2 6.2/ 13.5 5.7
50-75 in 5th(man) 80-120kmh	7.1/ 6.5	7.3/ 6.7	7.1/ 6.5	7.3/ 6.7
Maximum speed	Man- 174/177mph Tip- 171/174mph	Man- 174/ 177mph Tip- 171/ 174mph	Man -174/ 177mph Tip- 171/ 174mph	Man-174/ 177r Tip-171/ 174m
Urban Combined mpg	Man- 23.9/25.5 Tip- 23.5/25	23.9/25.4 23.5/25	23.5/25 22.8 /23.8	23.5/25 22.8 /23.8
Wheels/Tyres	Standard/All C2/C4/pre & facelift F-205/50 ZR 17 R-255/40 ZR 17	Optional/All C2/C4/pre-facelift 225/40 ZR 18 265/35 ZR 18	Optional/All C2/C4/ Facelift F-225/40ZR-18 R-285/30ZR18	
Brakes	4 piston calipers Discs F-318mm & R-299mm, Drilled/ventilated, ABS standard.	4 piston calipers Discs F-318mm & R-299mm, Drilled/ventilated, ABS standard	4 piston calipers Discs F-318mm & R-299mm, Drilled/ventilated, ABS standard.	4 piston calipe Discs F-318m R-299mm, Drilled/ventilat standard.
Drag coefficient/C$_d$	0.30	0.30	0.30	0.30
Transmission	6 speed manual/ 5speed Tiptronic Rear wheel drive	6 speed manual/ 5speed Tiptronic Rear wheel drive	6 speed manual/ 5speed Tiptronic 4-wheel drive	6 speed manu 5speed Tiptro 4 wheel drive

Dimensions- ALL C2/C4/Targa-
Length: 4430mm Width: 1765mm /1770mm
Height :1305mm
Track: 17-inch wheels 1455/1500 mm
17-inch 1465/1500mm 18-inch1465/1480)

TANK CAPACITY
(All 996 RHD models)
64 litres/14 gallons
GT3/GT3RS (LHD): 89 litres
(RHD cars are 64 litres)

BOOTSPACE
C2 130 litres
C4/4S/Turbo
100 litres.
GT2/3- 110 lit

rmance/ mpg / wheels & tyres / brakes / drag co-efficient Cd / dimensions & capacities.
igures in RED are for 'facelift' models.
arket cars offer approximately 5bhp (4kW) less than the European equivalents quoted
ghout the tables. Left-hand drive tank capacity is 90-litres.

	C4S	Turbo	GT3	
3596cc	3596cc	3600cc twin turbo inter-cooled	3600cc F-3800cc	3600cc twin turbo inter-cooled
/320bhp at n 273lbft) at n	235kW/320bhp at 6800rpm 370Nm/273 lbft) at 4250rpm	420BHP at 6000rpm , 560Nm /413lbft 2700-4600rpm.	360/381bhp at 7200/ 7,400rpm 370Nm 273/ 284lbft at 5000rpm	456/483bhp@ 5700rpm- 620/640Nm (457lbft/472lbft) 3500-4500rpm
70kg	man/tip 1470/1525kg (Cabrio 1565/1620kg)	man/tip 1540/1585kg (Cabrio 1660/1700kg)	1350kg 1380kg	1440kg 1420kg
hp/ 193lbft hp/ 186lbft	M-218bhp/ 186lbft T- 210bhp/ 179lbft Cab M:204bhp 174lbft Cab T:197bhp 168lbft	M-273bhp/269lbft T- 265bhp/ 260lbft Cab M:253bhp 249lbft Cab T:247bhp 243lbft	M-267bhp/202lb ft 276bhp/206lb ft No Tiptronic	M-316bhp/317lb ft 340bhp/332lb ft No Tiptronic
.4 4	5.1/11.3Cab5.3/11.8 5.6/12.3Cab5.9/13.4	4.2/ 9.3 Cab4.3/ 9.5 4.9/10.4 Cab4.9/10.7 (Turbo S 4.2/ 9)	4.8/ 10.2 4.5/ 9.4 No Tiptronic	4.1/8.5 4/ 8.3 No Tiptronic
	6.7/ 7.2 Cab	4.8/ 5.0 Cab 4.9 Turbo S	6.7/ 6.5	n/a/ 4.3
77mph 74 mph.	M-174mph (& Cab) T-171mph (& Cab)	M-190mph (&.Cab) T-185mph (&.Cab)	187/190mph	196/198mph
	24.8 Coupé & Cab. 23.35 Cab/ 23.2	21.9 (Coupé & Cab) 20.3 (Coupé & Cab)	21.9 No Tiptronic	21.9 No Tiptronic
	F-225/40ZR18 R-295/30ZR18	F-225/40ZR18 R-295/30ZR18	225/235/40ZR 18 285/295/30 ZR 18	F-235/40Z R 18 R-315/30Z R 18
calipers -318mm & m, ventilated, ndard.	4-piston calipers Discs 4 x 330mm, drilled/ ventilated, ABS standard.	4-piston calipers Discs 4x 330mm, drilled/ ventilated, ABS standard.	4-piston calipers Discs 4 x 330 mm drilled & ventilated. (front: 6-piston/ 350 mm disc) ABS.	6-piston calipers front & 4-piston rear , Discs 4 x 350mm Ceramic, drilled & ventilated, ABS.
	0.30	0.31	0.30	0.34
manual/ Tiptronic eel drive	6-speed manual/ 5-speed Tiptronic 4-wheel drive	6-speed manual/ 5-speed Tiptronic 4-wheel drive	6-speed manual only. Rear wheel drive	6-speed manual only. Rear wheel drive
	DimensionsTurbo/C4S Length: 4435mm Width: 1830mm Height: 1295mm Track: F-1472mm R-1528mm.		GT2: Length: 4446/4450mm Width: 1830mm, Height :1275mm. (Track: F-1485/1495mm R- 1520mm) GT3 Length: 4430/4435mm W: 1765/1,770mm H : 1270/1,275mm (Track: F-1475/1485mm R-1495/1485mm)	

1998 911 Carrera Cabriolet

Model changes year by year

In 1997 Porsche introduced one of the most major overhauls of the 911 range with the introduction of the 996 series. Larger and more refined, the new 911 was also lighter and more powerful than the earlier models. And to meet changing world markets, the 996 was also the first 911 in 34 years to feature a water-cooled engine. This section examines the 996 specification in more detail and considers its ongoing development.

Bodyshell

The zinc-dipped steel 911 bodyshell was completely redesigned for the 996, and at the time, exceeded all statutory crash protection requirements. The classic rear engine layout was retained, but everything else about the design was brought into the 21st century. The structural design featured a new crash protection system (patented by Porsche) at the front of the car combined with high tensile boron-steel side impact protection. The first 996s came with driver and front passenger airbag protection. For the 1998 model year Porsche Side Impact Protection (POSIP) with side airbags was offered as an option and became standard the following year.

One of the 996's more notable steps forward is its more roomy cabin, with more space for the rear occupants. Twin front radiators (ahead of the front wheels) allowed greater front compartment space.

The body was also far more rigid (around 45% stiffer in torsion) than the outgoing 993 series and despite being physically larger was also some 50 kg lighter. The sleek new outer shell captured key design cues from the traditional 911 form, but offered a completely fresh appearance. It was far more efficient aerodynamically, having a drag coefficient of 0.30 compared to the 993's 0.34. Lift over the front and rear axles was also reduced by having a degree of aerodynamic ground effect under the car and a rear spoiler that extended automatically. This popped up at speeds greater than 75mph (120km/h) and retracted at 37mph (60km/h).

The front luggage area was a quite different shape to the outgoing 911s. Now there was a deep cavity ahead of the emergency wheel. For the first time, proper suitcases could be carried in a 911!

The first 996 model was the Carrera 2, defined by its rear wheel drive only transmission. On the 996, like every other 911 before it, the engine is mounted behind the rear wheels, with clutch and transaxle gearbox ahead. This isn't ideal for weight distribution (although modern suspension and tyres have largely overcome the disadvantages) the layout does allow maximum space for the cabin and luggage bay.

The Carrera bodyshell was designed to accommodate both rear-wheel and all-wheel drive systems, with the Carrera 4 being introduced in late 1998. Visually there is little to differentiate the C4, aside from the titanium coloured badges and brake callipers, plus unique wheels if the standard 17-inchers were retained.

The Cabriolet was introduced in July 1998, and featured a convertible top that could be retracted in just 20 seconds. All 996 Cabriolets came with a hard-top as standard. The Cabriolet features reinforced windscreen pillars and automatically-deployed roll-over protection housed behind the rear seats.

By chopping off the top of the car and reinforcing the chassis, Cabriolets are both less rigid and heavier then their coupé equivalent – a factor to remember if you are seeking a car for best performance. As with all softops you need a wind deflector to reduce back draft however, the system Porsche use prevents the use of the rear seats. Another not so pleasing feature is the rather nasty plastic rear window. The roof design was significantly improved for the 2002 model year, with a (heated) glass rear window and remote operation (in just 20 seconds!) from the key fob. The roof could now also be raised and lowered whilst moving at low speeds.

The 'wide-body' Carrera 4S was launched in September 2001 in coupé form. Looking like the Turbo, but with the Carrera engine, these models further extended the wide variety of choice that has become a characteristic of the 996 range. In October 2003, the C4S was also offered as a Cabriolet.

Launched in September 2001 for the 2002 model year, the facelift Carrera models offered improvements in aerodynamic efficiency, increased rigidly & crash safety.

The 996 version of the Targa also launched for the 2002 model year. Although based on the stiffer coupé body, it is still 70kg heavier than a standard Carrera 2!

The extra light let into the cabin by the full glass roof makes the interior much brighter and more pleasant, and the new model also added a 911 first with it's very practical rear opening hatch.

With the Targa you don't get the full wind-in-your-hair, exhaust in your ears experience of a Cabriolet (which is only slightly more expensive) or the benefits of the lighter, more agile (and far cheaper) coupé.

What you do get is basically a very expensive large sunroof, which can be noisy and which, when open, will obscure the rear view. Having said this, if you are buying used, the price differential to the coupé will be far less (if not eliminated). At that point, a Targa can make a lot of sense if you seek a Carrera that offers both good cabin security and open-air driving.

If the standard look wasn't enough, special body kits or interiors could be ordered to make the car that bit more special. Porsche's in-house custom equipment and tuning business is called Porsche Exclusive. The Exclusive options list is huge, and many 996s have been specified from the factory with items such as walnut or carbon/aluminium trimmed interiors or special aero kits to make the exterior look more sophisticated or aggressive.

Most popular for the early pre-facelift cars was the Cup Aerokit, making a standard Carrera look like a series 1 GT3. The later Aerokit offered a large fixed rear spoiler and lower painted front splitter and proved popular on the C4S & Turbo, adding further aggression.

Engine

The 996 features a water-cooled flat-6 cylinder engine, breaking with the 911 tradition of cooling the cylinders by air. Increased exhaust emissions and noise standards dictated the new cooling method. Nevertheless, the engine offers a marked improvement in every operating regime compared to the older unit.

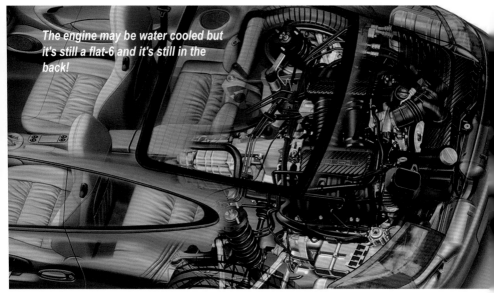

The engine may be water cooled but it's still a flat-6 and it's still in the back!

At launch, the capacity of the all-alloy design was 3,387cc, producing 300bhp (221kW) at 6800rpm with a revolution limit set at fully 7250rpm. Maximum torque was 350Nm (258 lb.ft) at 4600rpm. Compared to the 993's larger 3.6-litre engine this was a 10 per cent improvement in maximum power.

The 7 bearing crankshaft is located in a cast aluminium alloy crankcase that also houses the integrated engine oil reservoir. Not having an external oil tank for the dry-sump lubrication system meant the size and quantity of the oil pumps could be reduced, as well as the pipework, with savings all-round on weight.

The Lokasil-coated cylinders are cast into place in each half of the crankcase, with plenty of space in between for future capacity increases!

The new cooling method has permitted 4 valves per cylinder (not possible with an air-cooled engine because the upper valves shield the lower valves), with fully integrated coolant passages cast into the cylinder heads. The double overhead camshafts are driven (as before) by chains from the crankshaft.

The new engine featured Porsche's patented Variocam technology that, under control of the Motronic 5.2 engine management system, adjusts the inlet valve timing according to engine speed. The Motronic system also controls the coil-on-plug ignition and the sequential multipoint fuel injection. The system has cylinder-specific anti-knock control, allowing a wide range of gasoline grades to be used.

The engine has computerised On-Board Diagnostics (OBD), a laptop plug-in fault-finding facility to ease the mechanic's task.

A two-stage induction system maximises cylinder filling and engine torque while also producing the much-loved induction roar, so characteristic of earlier 911s.

The 2002 models were subject to a major upgrade in engine specification. These engines developed a maximum power of 320bhp (235kW) and featured the Variocam Plus technology first seen on the Turbo. The inlet valve tappets are 'switchable', so that depending on engine speed, they are operated by different camshaft profiles. This is a more complex variation on variable inlet valve timing that further optimises torque (to a maximum of 370Nm (273lb.ft), fuel consumption and exhaust emissions across the revolution range.

The 996 was fitted with two separate exhaust systems (one for each bank) each with a "twin-metal" catalytic converter and twin Lambda probes.

Porsche increased the volume of the 996 exhaust system, first for 1999 and then again for 2002. Nevertheless, a full Sports system is a popular choice among enthusiasts.

Porsche offer their own system, which avoids warranty issues, is competitively priced and even has a switch that can put the sound back to standard (although if you opt for the switch it is very costly to fit).

If you are a trackday fan beware the noise restrictions as most systems can push the car over the limit, (which makes the Porsche switch even more useful). If you prefer an after-market system, be careful not to select one that is too noisy. Some of the extreme systems can make the car sound like a tractor outside. Check out resonance levels, warranty and build quality with the seller. And make sure you keep the original system for re-sale.

Porsche introduced an (expensive) optional power kit that basically added about 20bhp (25bhp for the 2002-onwards cars) to the naturally aspirated cars and 30bhp to the Turbo. They add a slightly more aggressive feel to the cars.

The X-50 power upgrade for the turbo has proved particularly sought after in the used market, as much of the original purchase premium has now gone. You can enjoy an increase to 450bhp and the most powerful "official" Turbo for little more than a standard car. It's well worth seeking out!

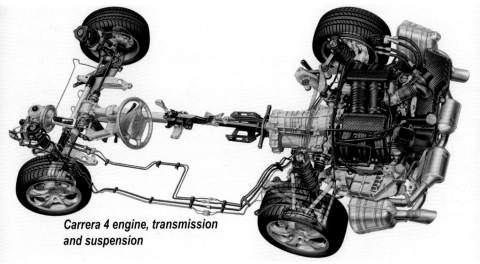

Carrera 4 engine, transmission and suspension

Transmission

From launch, the 996 was available with either a new-design 6-speed manual gearbox (standard) or the optional 5 speed Tiptronic automatic.

The 6-speed manual is fast, precise and has a good feel. It offers well-chosen ratios (2nd will rev to 72mph, 3rd to 103mph!) that maximise the car's performance. Transmission refinement was improved with a dual-mass flywheel to cut out gearbox rattle and humming in the drive train. A new cable-operated gearshift mechanism prevents engine vibrations reaching the gear lever.

The automatic Tiptronic S system offers two modes. The first is the 'intelligent' automatic mode with 5 different gear-shift patterns (ranging from economy to sport) that are selected according to your driving style. Unlike other automatics, the system is also designed not to change up before a corner, to aid stability and performance.

When the conditions or mood takes you, there is also a manual mode. By moving the lever across the gate, the gears can be changed by pressing buttons on the steering wheel, or by 'tipping' (hence the name) the shift lever backwards or forwards. Porsche claim the changes take around only 0.2 seconds and it certainly is as near-seamless as you could wish.

For the 1999 model year, Porsche unveiled the Carrera 4. As the name suggested this featured Porsches own 'intelligent' 4-wheel drive system. Power is split between front and rear wheels through a viscous coupling. A minimum of 5 per cent of the engine's power is applied to the front wheels, around 35 per cent in normal driving, with a

'Facelift' headlamp on 2002-onwards Carreras

Carrera engine bay

maximum of 40 per cent in extreme driving conditions.

Truth is, you will be hard pressed to tell the difference between C2 and C4 unless you are familiar with 911s. The biggest benefit of the 911's engine weight slung out of the rear wheels is fantastic traction. This means even in streaming wet conditions you can floor a Carrera 2 (in a straight line) and simply slingshot up the road. The 4-wheel drive improves traction not overall grip.

Nevertheless, the extra weight of the 4-wheel drive system at the front of the car does give the C4 a slightly more 'tied down' and stable feel, with less of the 'nose bobbing' which has always been a characteristic of the two wheel drive 911s. There is also no doubt that extra front-end traction can help improve the 911's (already mighty) wet weather cornering ability. It also seems to reduce the understeer that the standard C2 can exhibit when pushed hard.

In addition to all-wheel drive, the C4 was the first Porsche to feature Porsche Stability Management (PSM) – a fantastic cutting edge traction control system. Bosch's Motronic's ME7.2 engine management system allowed for control of the new electronic throttle and works with the PSM system to vary the drive to each wheel.

PSM brakes each individual wheel to reduce under- and oversteer in extreme conditions. This very sophisticated safety system utilises wheel speed, yaw velocity, lateral acceleration and steering angle sensors to ensure an accurate response and only intervenes when you really need it. Standard equipment on the C4, PSM would eventually be offered as an option on the C2 from 2000. However, it appeared to be even more effective when combined with the 4-wheel drive system.

The earlier Carrera 2 was also available with an optional Traction Control system (pre-2000), but this was much more intrusive and less efficient than the excellent PSM (being unable to brake each individual wheel separately) and although useful on a wet road, it isn't the "must have" option that PSM is!

The downside of the C4's sophisticated transmission is that it is heavier and hence slightly slower, but most will find it hard to notice much difference in a straight drag!

As a post-script, it is also worth noting that the 4-wheel drive system removes a big chunk of boot space (about a third) and of course, you can pay around 10 per cent extra for the C4 over the C2 (although PSM would account for part of that).

The C4 will also have slightly higher running costs, with more wear on front tyres, brakes, suspension etc. My own personal thoughts are that if you were buying new then a C2 probably makes more sense from a value viewpoint. If you are buying used, where the price differential is closer, then the C4 makes a great case for itself.

Suspension and steering

The 996 offered an evolution of the earlier 993's suspension arrangement, with coil springs over double-tube gas shock absorbers and direct-geared tube-type anti-roll bars front and rear. The wheelbase was lengthened by 80mm over the 993 series to 2350mm (92.5 inches), in order to improve stability, optimise suspension characteristics and reduce pitching. The ride quality and suspension performance was also improved by reducing the unsprung weight (the wheels, hubs and brake assemblies).

The front suspension features MacPherson principle struts with "floating" aluminium control arms. A longitudinal control arm and an additional transverse control arm are connected by a flexible rubber bushing, offering extremely accurate control of the wheel position.

The rear suspension offers the race proven Light-Stable-Agile (LSA) multi-link design mounted on an alloy sub-frame. The system can accommodate a maximum lateral load well in excess of 1G and has

The hardtop for the 911 Carrera Cabriolet was a standard item with the car

geometry that promotes reduced understeer during high speed cornering. The LSA rear axle virtually buried for good the legend that 911s were nervous and tail-happy.

The power-assisted rack-and-pinion steering is an evolution of the proven system used on earlier models. Although slightly less direct than before, it still offered a generous and responsive 3 turns lock-to-lock. Importantly, the steering still retained the superb weighting and feel for which the 911 has become renowned. The turning circle was slightly increased to a still-excellent 10.6 metres (just under 35ft).

The standard Carrera suspension offers great everyday driving and touring comfort, but the Sports chassis (lowered by 10mm and standard on the C4S and Turbo) will give a more focused driver's car. Although the ride is less comfortable, the firmer suspension transforms the car when it is pushed hard, reducing body roll, pitch, float and understeer.

For track day enthusiasts there is the Sports chassis lowered by 30mm (standard on the GT3). But be warned, this is rock hard! Although you'll need to watch your fillings on a country road – it is fantastic on a smooth road or the racetrack.

Brakes, wheels and tyres

Porsche's reputation for producing some of the most effective fade-free braking systems available was further reinforced with the 996. An increase in disc size combined with improved ventilation and reduced weight saw the latest series 911 stop faster and more consistently than ever before.

The brakes are cross-drilled and internally ventilated steel discs all round in 318mm (12.5-inch) diameter at the front and 299mm (11.8-inch) diameter at the rear. The calipers are a 4-piston aluminium alloy monobloc design. Wheel locking under heavy braking is controlled by the extremely effective Bosch 3-channel ABS system.

The front brakes are air-cooled by ducts that take their air from openings that are positioned under the front of the car.

Porsche also offered the option of ceramic brakes (The Porsche Ceramic Composite Brake (PCCB) system was standard on the GT2 & Turbo S), but there have been durability issues & they are VERY expensive to replace. If you are looking at a car with PCCBs fitted be sure to take expert advice on their condition.

The standard wheels on both the Carrera 2 and Carrera 4 models are 17-inch diameter

The 996 was fitted with several wheels throughout its life, and the designs can differ whether they are the standard 17-inch versions or the optional 18-inch types. Not shown here is the 10-'Y' spoke 18-inch Sport Classic 2 wheel

The photo (above) shows the optional Turbo-look 17-inch alloy wheel fitted to the car at the time of its launch in 1997

At the top left is the 18-inch, 2-piece Sport Design alloy wheel fitted to the early (1999-2000) GT3s and available as an option on later Carreras.

The wheel on the lower left is the optional 18-inch 5-spoke design offered for the 2002 Carreras with ZR rated tyres in sizes 205/50 front and 255/40 at the rear. The optional fit were 18-inch wheels with 225/40 front and 285/30 rear tyres. The Carrera 4S has 18-inch wheels, with 225/40 front and 295/30 rear tyres.

18-inch wheels greatly improve the sporting look of the car and add more cornering grip, although they do reduce the degree of adjustability and the ride quality. You have to take great care not to scuff them against high kerbs. I think these are a 'must have' option for the 996.

The 18-inch Turbo wheels (from the previous serious 993 Turbo) were most popular on early 996s. The choice widened to include 'SportClassic 2' (Y cross-spoke shaped) the GT3 lookalike 2-piece Sport Design (but beware the studs, they are a nightmare to clean!) and more recently, the slim 5 spoke 18" Carrera wheel (that offers a lighter and easier to clean design).

Be sure to check that the wheels on your used 996 are original Porsche items, there are many cheaper imitations that may not wear as well or be as light!

On all models, an emergency-only spare tyre is mounted in the front compartment.

Interior

One thing most people tend to agree with is that the 993 series interior was in desperate need of updating and modernisation. With the 996, Porsche took the opportunity to share the major components of a completely revised interior with the new Boxster model – a decision that undoubtedly brought economies of scale to the production cost.

Although the end result is perhaps too similar to the Boxster for many eyes

The multi-spoke wheel as fitted to the new generation GT3 from 2004

(despite a higher standard specification), the all-new interior certainly transformed the 911 interior's functionality, design and ergonomics. The instruments and controls are far more intuitive and easy to use.

The only blot on this improvement is the analogue speedometer (on the left of the main instrument cluster). This is virtually useless and you find the digital read-out far more useful. This may seem strange at first, but you soon get used to it.

The larger overall size of the 996 also allowed for more interior space, with around 190mm (7.5 inches) more internal width, plus more front head room, a larger front compartment and more rear storage behind the back seats. Nevertheless, for longer journeys, the rear seats still remain only suitable for small children.

The standard option specification varies between countries, as an example right-hand drive UK cars (code C16) were built to one of the highest standard specifications. Receiving a top tinted windscreen with built-in antenna and (with the exception of some of the early 1997 cars) a full leather interior, metallic paint, air-conditioning and the highest specification alarm system within the basic price.

The interior of the 911 Carrera, These seats have electric adjustment of front/back position and recline

The rear seating area is unexpectedly roomy. The seat backs fold flat to allow extra luggage to be carried

While the left-hand drive American market cars did not receive full leather as standard, there are other detail changes such as different bumpers to meet differing national legislation. This is why it is important to check the car's country code if there are any doubts as to its specification and origin.

All 996s came with a 2-year warranty, a basic stereo, electric windows (with one touch facility) and exterior mirrors (that are, like the rear screen, heated), dual speed wipers with intermittent wipe and heated washer jets, split fold rear seats, twin airbags, an alarm immobiliser and the driver's seat with an electrically operated back recline.

Equipment and accessories

There is a large range of options available for the 996. Nevertheless, it's important to understand that while options generally add desirability to a used car, they only rarely add value. The factory options fitted can be identified from the car's Vehicle Identification Label (VIL) and the Options list starting on page 36. Well consider some of the more sought-after options.

Sports seats look good and provide extra support in hard cornering, but they can be rather firm for longer journeys. They are not to be confused with Sport bucket seats which offer the ultimate lateral support but cannot be tilted for access to the rear or adjusted for height (without a visit to a dealer). Seats can be ordered with heating and a more expensive option is full electric-adjustment with a 3-position memory facility (standard on the Turbo).

If the car you are looking at has the ruffled leather option, be aware that the leather can stretch and sag after extended use.

The CD changer and aftermarket sat-nav player are concealed behind the rear seat back on this Turbo

Among other sought-after options are cruise control (useful in this age of speed detectors!), the On-Board Computer (featuring mpg (or l/100km) remaining range, average speed, outside air temperature and more). Note that the computer became standard on 2002 models (with more options and a larger display).

Litronic/Bi-Xenon headlamps are a very desirable extra as they claim to offer twice the illumination of the regular Halogen lights.

Porsche Communications Management (PCM) is a sought after (but expensive) option, that will help ease of re-sale. The system offers one module that controls a number of functions, complete with its own built-in full colour screen. First and foremost is a very good satellite navigation system. PCM also controls the in-car entertainment system, a more sophisticated trip computer and provides a good quality hands-free cellphone (with the handset as an optional extra).

The PCM system was further upgraded for the 2003 model year to PCM2 (standard on the Turbo from 2004). If you are buying an early car you will find PCM hard to find as sat-nav wasn't that popular at that time. It is far more likely to be included in the specification of a post-2002 car.

It is worth noting that Porsche do not appear to have supported updates for the Navigation system very well. Particularly on the older (pre-2003) cars, where the mapping is now years out of date!

The early cars came with a very basic cassette radio, while later there was the choice of a single play CD or Minidisc. If you enjoy a decent stereo you will want to buy a car with an upgraded system. The first level of upgrade was the sound pack (extra speakers and an up rated amplifier). Earlier cars also offered an excellent system called DSP (Digital Sound Processing) by Nokia. More recent versions offer the Bose system (standard on the Turbo for the 2002 model year) as the top upgrade. Porsche also offer a 6 CD changer for the front compartment

and if this isn't fitted, many will have the wiring ready to fit it.

Up to 2001 the standard steering wheel was a bulky four-spoke (rather ugly) design and because you can only adjust the wheel fore and aft it was difficult to prevent it fouling the knees of a taller driver. The optional Sports wheel not only looks nicer but is also a little smaller and easier to use.

You can also lift the appearance of the interior by adding alloy, leather, carbon and wood to a whole host of trim parts, thanks to the Porsche Exclusive custom range of equipment. The handbrake and gear lever upgrade is one of the most popular and attractive, as is having the Porsche crest stamped into the seat backs.

There are too many Exclusive options to cover them all here, including uprated engines (powerkits) body/aero kits and much more.

The Porsche Communication Management (PCM) system controls satellite navigation with mobile telephone, radio and CD player

Special models

GT3

The GT3 was Porsche's answer to those who suggested the new generation 911s might have gone soft.

The suspension is 30mm lower (compared to the standard Carrera) and the car has much of the non-essential accessories and equipment stripped out to provide a more raw, focused driving experience. Ironically, the GT3 actually weighs more than a standard Carrera 2, because it utilises the stiffer body shell of the current Carrera 4.

Launched in 1999 (for the 2000 model year, but not in the US) the GT3 offered a useful step up in output to 360bhp (265kW) from a higher revving (to 7600 revs) engine that can (as with the Turbo) trace much of its origins to the GT1 race car.

The GT3 may not be ideal as an everyday driver, but it is perfect for fast cross-country or trackday work. The firm, near-race car handling won't appeal to every driver, particularly the car's susceptibility to tram-lining on uneven or rutted roads. But put it on a racetrack and it is in its element. A Turbo may reign supreme on the road, but on track it rolls and floats in comparison with the GT3.

The maximum speed is 187mph and acceleration from standstill to 62mph is 4.8 seconds.

The first series of GT3s, delivered in 1999 and 2000 came in Comfort versions (just about usable for everyday driving) and Club Sport versions (which Porsche describe as suitable for the aspiring racing enthusiast). The latter came with full roll-over cage, fire extinguisher and front and rear strut supports. It is a very basic, but very quick track car.

This first generation GT3 series have

"The GT3 was Porsche's answer to those who said the 911 had gone soft"

held strong residual values because it was a limited edition, but the new car launched for the 2004 model year is a full production model. It was also officially available within the US market for the first time.

The new 'facelift' model has maximum power improved from 360bhp to 381bhp (280kW), and with improved aerodynamic efficiency has a top speed of 190mph.

The standing start acceleration time to 62mph is just 4.5 seconds, but is notable for having a slightly better ride on normal roads.

The first series GT3 had 330mm (13-ins) diameter discs (clamped by 4 piston calipers all round, the same as the Turbo). The facelift model benefits from an increase in the size of the front brakes (which take most of the strain) to 350mm (13.8ins – and now bigger than the Turbo), with 6-piston even-bigger 'Big Red' calipers that improve the contact area by no less than 40 per cent. The Porsche ceramic (PCCB) brakes are an option, saving no fewer than 18kg in unsprung weight.

Turbo

Launched in 2000, the 996 Turbo is, point-to-point, quite simply one of the fastest road cars on the planet.

The 420bhp (309kW) twin-turbo, twin-intercooled engine is derived from the Le Mans-winning racing GT1 and has VarioCam Plus variable valve timing technology. Like the earlier 993 Turbo, it has full-time 4-wheel drive and compared to the Carrera the new car has stiffer suspension and more powerful brakes.

Existing Carrera owners may ask if the Turbo is worth that much more than a Carrera 4S, but the Turbo has so much more to offer than even the C4S!

Visually the Turbo is defined by its side air vents in the rear wings, electrically-operated (on dual rams) rear spoiler and a lip (splitter) on the front spoiler.

The standard equipment also includes powerful Bi-Xenon headlamps (with integral cleaning) a standard fit sunroof and special 18-inch hollow spoke lightweight "Turbo 2" alloy wheels. Inside you could specify

One of the fastest road cars on the planet - the 420bhp (309kW) 911 Turbo

sports seats as a no cost option (NCO) and the standard seats came with full electronic adjustment and driver's seat memory. Be aware that if you choose a car with sports seats, it won't come with the full electric/ memory package! The stereo was upgraded to a top of the range package and, from the '02 model year, this was made by Bose. In the same year the auto-dim mirror with rain sensor also became standard. From the 04-model year the PCM satellite navigation package was standard. The Turbo also benefited from all the facelift 996's other features.

Porsche's flagship is still a fantastic driver's car. The sheer power is addictive and the cornering and stopping capabilities are exceptional.

The 911 Turbo is an all-weather supercar that you can really use every day.

911 GT3 RS

Based on the earlier GT3 Club Sport, the 2004 model RS was announced in August 2003. The power unit is the standard facelift GT3 381bhp (280kW), normally-aspirated flat-6. The addition of a single mass racing flywheel and a weight reduction of 20kg (despite the steel roll-over cage!) resulted in a slight improvement in top speed. The new RS received redesigned wheelhub assemblies, improved lateral control arms on the suspension and distinctive carbonfibre exterior mirrors and rear wing.

Acceleration to 62mph from standstill is achieved in 4.4 seconds and the maximum speed is 190mph. The RS is as minimalist as you can get in a modern 911 and really only suitable for sports driving. The cars were only delivered in white with either blue or red body decals and wheel centres.

2004 911 GT3 RS

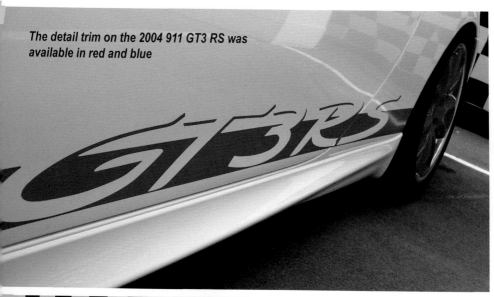

The detail trim on the 2004 911 GT3 RS was available in red and blue

911 GT2

The GT flagship is the GT2, a 462bhp (340kW) Turbo with rear-wheel drive only and no Porsche Stability Management (like the GT3). This 197mph road-rocket also enjoys a 100kg weight advantage on the regular 911 Turbo, having an unladen weight of 1440kg.

The GT2 is the first Porsche production car to be fitted as standard with the Porsche Ceramic Composite Brakes (PCCB), with discs that weigh 50 per cent less than the steel equivalents and offer more consistent friction characteristics under heavy braking loads and longer service life.

The GT2 doesn't have the practicality of a 911 Turbo for everyday or long distance touring use. The front Sports seats are fixed, which largely denies use of the area behind them. The most extreme version of the GT2 is the Club Sport version, which is ready to use in competition.

A 2003 911 GT2 in Basalt black metallic

The combination of all that instant turbocharged power, just two wheels to transmit it and further up-rated, rock-hard suspension make the GT2 an extreme adrenaline-pumping experience. Because of the way the Turbo engine delivers such a big hit of instant torque (a maximum of 560Nm (413lb.ft) from 2700rpm to 4600rpm!), it makes the car far less easy to drive than a GT3 and perhaps a step too far for some.

The GT2 was also up rated for the 2004 model year, with an increased output of 483bhp (355kW) and along with aerodynamic and drivetrain improvements offered a top speed of 199mph and a 0 to 62mph time of 4.0 seconds (an improvement of 0.1 seconds). The car is fitted with new GT3-look wheels and carbonfibre spoilers and exterior mirrors.

We would advise owners not to use the GT2 for track work as the design of the ceramic brakes is specific for all conditions

This GT2 has Porsche Exclusive carbon trim to the dash and centre console

of road use only. Heavy track use can overheat and ruin them.

Oddly, the residuals on the GT2 have not been strong – perhaps because the 911 Turbo is so suited for general road use and the GT3 ideal for the track. The GT2 doesn't quite work perfectly in either role, but it's certainly a fantastic and awe-inspiring car to own and drive!

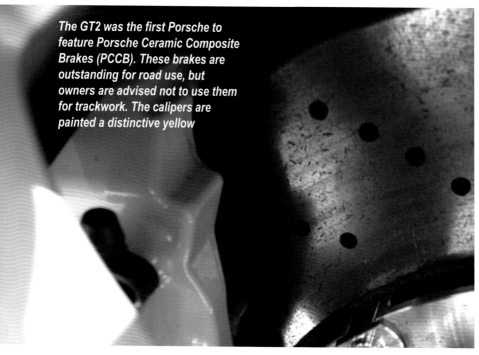

The GT2 was the first Porsche to feature Porsche Ceramic Composite Brakes (PCCB). These brakes are outstanding for road use, but owners are advised not to use them for trackwork. The calipers are painted a distinctive yellow

Carrera 4S

Launched in the same year as the facelift models (September 2001 for the 2002 model year), the Carrera 4S is inspired by the aggressive appearance of the Turbo.

The C4S continues the 'wide-body' fashion in 911s that was so popular with the 993 and earlier models. Nevertheless, this use of the designation 'S' shouldn't be confused with the Tiptronic S or the later Turbo S models. The Tiptronic 'S' denotes cars with steering wheel push-buttons and the Turbo 'S' a higher power pack. If you find it confusing, don't worry, so does everybody else!

The Carrera 4S has the Turbo's larger intakes in the front bumper and the broader (60mm or 2.4-inch) rear wings (but without the intakes).

The car retains the regular Carrera's 320bhp (235kW) normally-aspirated engine, but shares the Turbo's 4-wheel drive system complete with that car's excellent suspension and brakes.

Although around 5 per cent more expensive than a standard Carrera 4 when new, the C4S offers a significant number of desirable extra options.

The specification includes 18-inch Turbo-look 2 wheels with wider track and rear tyres, the Turbo body kit with rear reflector strip, the Turbo's more powerful brakes (with 330mm, 13-inch diameter steel discs all round), 10mm (0.4-inch) lowered Sports chassis, full electrically-adjustable seats and the Porsche sound pack.

In those markets where the Carrera 2

The 911 Carrera 4S adopted the Turbo's excellent underpinnings and much of its eye-catching visual appearance

didn't receive full leather as standard, this was also given to the C4S. Full leather is defined as covering areas such as the dash, door trims etc., not just the front seat facings.

Although the C4S is heavier than a standard C4, the combination of its wider track and tyres, the 10mm Sports chassis and standard fit PSM (Porsche Stability Management) make it nearly unbeatable point to point (unless you have a Turbo!). Combine this with its chunkier more aggressive look and you can see why it has been such a big seller for Porsche.

Importantly, early experience suggests the C4S models also offer the best residual levels of all the 996 models.

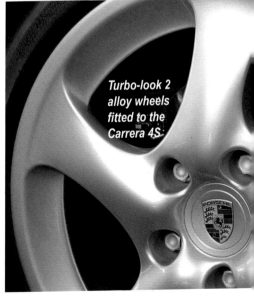

Turbo-look 2 alloy wheels fitted to the Carrera 4S

911 Carrera 40th anniversary edition

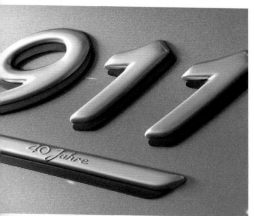

Anniversary editions

The 2000 Millennium was a limited run of uniquely specified Carrera 4 models (with PSM) in Violet chrome metallic paint, Equipment included Litronic headlights, chromed Turbo-look alloy wheels, heated memory seats, PCM, DSP sound, sunroof, 3-spoke steering wheel, reverse-painted dials, cruise control, OBC, CD changer and a burr maple/natural leather interior.

For the 2004 model year, Porsche released another special edition, this time an altogether more serious proposition commemorating the 911's (remarkable) 40 years in production.

This special certainly wasn't cheap, but included a range of valuable options. These included an extra 25bhp (19kW), a Sports chassis (firmer springs, shock absorbers and anti-roll bars), Porsche Stability Management (PSM) and a limited slip differential (to help traction out of tighter corners).

The appearance was improved with a Turbo-look body kit, chromed wheels (the 18-inch diameter Carrera items), electric sunroof, Litronic headlights, heated sports seats that were given silvered backs. The final touch was a silvered centre tunnel. The car carried a '911 40 Jahre' badge on the engine cover, which was repeated at the base of the central dash area.

Turbo S

Announced even after the new 997 had made its debut in June 2004, the Turbo S suggested that certain versions of the 'older' model were likely to remain in production for a while yet. The new models were sold from the start of the 2005 model year.

The Turbo S came in Coupé and Cabriolet versions and came with a (Porsche Exclusive originated) Performance package that adds 30bhp (22kW) and takes maximum power to 450bhp (331kW) and maximum torque to a massive 620Nm (457lb.ft).

The cars come with PCCB (Porsche Ceramic Composite Brakes), cruise control, PCM (Porsche Communication Management, the sat-nav), CD autochanger, GT-silver painted 18-inch Turbo 2 alloy wheels and reverse-painted aluminium faced instrument dials.

The Turbo S models also introduced a new exterior colour, namely olive green metallic.

Both models could be ordered with 5-speed Tiptronic automatic transmission or the manual 6-speed gearbox.

The 911 Turbo S coupé (rear) and Cabriolet

Production information (1997 to 2004)
Model types and chassis numbers
The following information is derived from a number of sources and serves to clarify the basic models and their model years.

Table notes
The first models listed for each year are those specified for Germany and Rest of World (RoW) markets, followed by the specific models for the USA (abbreviated to US).

The chassis numbers shown are industry standard 17-character Vehicle Identification Numbers (VIN). To illustrate what they mean, consider this typical US 911 Carrera 2 Cabriolet: WPOCA299_XS600001. WPO is the world make code for Porsche; CA2 is the US VSD code. The first VSD letter is the body type – A for coupé, C for a Cabriolet, D for Targa. The second VSD letter is the engine/transmission type – A for two wheel drive, B is for four wheel drive. The third VSD digit is the occupant safety system type – 0 for seat belts only, 1 for driver airbag, 2 for driver/passenger airbags. In other markets (like Europe) these three VSD characters are just left ZZZ (eg: WPOZZZ99ZXS6000061). Next in the chassis number are the first two digits of the model type (99) followed by a test number (on US models this NHTSA space is usually left blank and in RoW it's left as a Z) and the model year letter (V for 1997, W for 1998, X for 1999, Y for 2000). The model year letter changed to 1 in 2001, then 2 for 2002 etc. The 11th digit is the plant code: S for Stuttgart; next is the third digit of the type number (6) and the body/engine code (eg: 4 for Cabriolet, etc). The last 4 digits are the serial number. The 3rd digit of the engine number also corresponds with the model year letter eg: 66X00001 is a 1999 model. No distinction is made here between the Carrera 2 and Carrera 4 (although US models can be identified by the second VSD letter). The first 60 chassis numbers for each model are reserved for Porsche internal use.

Transmission type (2 or 4-wheel drive) and 2003-on 4S models are not defined in the chassis number. Note that Carrera 4 is 55kg heavier than Carrera 2.

For space reasons (there are a lot of 996 models!) apart from the standard 911 Carrera Coupé for the US we have shown only the Rest of World chassis number series. For the specific US chassis numbers, the VSD code can be worked out using the information above, and main chassis number differences are shown as footnotes to each year. Canada and Mexico models have same numbers as the US.

For Brazil specific models: 1998 and 1999 C2 coupés carry 9 at 13th digit followed by 8. The Brazil specific 1998 C4 coupé's 13th digit is 9 followed by 4, the 1999 C2 Cabriolet is 9 followed by 6 and the 1999 C4 Cabriolet has 9 followed by 8. After 1999, Brazil models used the same 13th/14th digit allocation as the US.

Model	Max power KW (Bhp)	Max torque Nm (lb.ft)	Weight kg	Chassis number series
1997				
911 Carrera	221 (300)	350 (258)	1320	WPOZZZ99ZVS600061-
911 Carrera US	221 (300)	350 (258)	1320	WPOAA299_VS620061-
1998				
911 Carrera	221 (300)	350 (258)	1320	WPOZZZ99ZWS600061-
911 Carrera US	221 (300)	350 (258)	1320	WPOAA299_WS620061-
911 Carrera Cabriolet	221 (300)	350 (258)	1395	WPOZZZ99ZWS640061-
(US Cabriolets have 5 at 13th digit)				
1999				
911 Carrera	221 (300)	350 (258)	1320	WPOZZZ99ZXS600061-
911 Carrera US	221 (300)	350 (258)	1320	WPOAA299_XS600061-
911 Carrera Cabriolet	221 (300)	350 (258)	1395	WPOZZZ99ZXS640061-
911 GT3	265 (360)	370 (273)	1350	WPOZZZ99ZXS690061-

Model	Max power KW (Bhp)	Max torque Nm (lb.ft)	Weight kg	Chassis number series
2000				
911 Carrera	221 (300)	350 (258)	1320	WPOZZZ99ZYS600061-
911 Carrera US	221 (300)	350 (258)	1320	WPOAA299_YS620061-
911 Carrera Cabriolet	221 (300)	350 (258)	1395	WPOZZZ99ZYS640061-
911 GT3	265 (360)	370 (273)	1350	WPOZZZ99ZYS690061-
911 Turbo	309 (420)	560 (413)	1540	WPOZZZ99ZYS680061-
2001				
911 Carrera	221 (300)	350 (258)	1320	WPOZZZ99Z1S600061-
911 Carrera US	221 (300)	350 (258)	1320	WPOAA299_1S620061-
911 Carrera Cabriolet	221 (300)	350 (258)	1395	WPOZZZ99Z1S640061-
911 Turbo	309 (420)	560 (413)	1540	WPOZZZ99Z1S680061-
GT2	340 (462)	620 (457)	1440	WPOZZZ99Z1S695061-
(US Turbos have 5 at 14th digit)				
2002				
911 Carrera	235 (320)	370 (273)	1345	WPOZZZ99Z2S600061-
911 Carrera US	235 (320)	370 (273)	1345	WPOAA299_2S620061-
911 Carrera 4S	235 (320)	370 (273)	1470	WPOZZZ99Z2S600061-
911 Carrera Cabriolet	235 (320)	370 (273)	1425	WPOZZZ99ZXS640061-
911 Targa	235 (320)	370 (273)	1415	WPOZZZ99Z2S630061-
911 Turbo	309 (420)	560 (413)	1540	WPOZZZ99Z2S680061-
GT2	340 (462)	620 (457)	1440	WPOZZZ99Z2S695061-
(US Targas have 5 at 14th digit, US GT2s have 6 at 14th digit)				
2003				
911 Carrera	235 (320)	370 (273)	1370	WPOZZZ99Z3S600061-
911 Carrera US	235 (320)	370 (273)	1370	WPOAA299_3S620061-
911 Carrera 4S	235 (320)	370 (273)	1495	WPOZZZ99Z3S600061-
911 Carrera Cabriolet	235 (320)	370 (273)	1450	WPOZZZ99Z3S640061-
911 Targa	235 (320)	370 (273)	1440	WPOZZZ99Z3S630061-
911 Turbo	309 (420)	560 (413)	1540	WPOZZZ99Z3S680061-
GT3	280 (381)	385 (284)	1380	WPOZZZ99Z3S690061-
GT2	340 (462)	620 (457)	1440	WPOZZZ99Z3S695061-
2004				
911 Carrera	235 (320)	370 (273)	1370	WPOZZZ99Z4S600061-
911 Carrera US	235 (320)	370 (273)	1370	WPOAA299_4S620061-
911 Carrera 4S	235 (320)	370 (273)	1495	WPOZZZ99Z4S600061-
911 Carrera 4S Cabrio	235 (320)	370 (273)	1565	WPOZZZ99Z4S640061-
911 Carrera Cabriolet	235 (320)	370 (273)	1450	WPOZZZ99Z4S640061-
911 Targa	235 (320)	370 (273)	1440	WPOZZZ99Z4S630061-
GT3	280 (381)	385 (284)	1380	WPOZZZ99Z4S690061-
GT3 RS	280 (381)	385 (284)	1330	WPOZZZ99Z4S690061-
911 Turbo	309 (420)	560 (413)	1590	WPOZZZ99Z4S680061-
911 Turbo Cabriolet	309 (420)	560 (413)	1660	WPOZZZ99Z4S670061-
GT2	355 (483)	640 (472)	1420	WPOZZZ99Z4S695061-

Year by year colours and interior choices

1997
External body colours
Black, Guards red, Pastel yellow, Glacier white, Ocean blue metallic, Zenith blue metallic, Arena red metallic, Arctic silver metallic, Ocean jade metallic, Black metallic, Mirage metallic, Vesuvio grey metallic
Interiors
Leather/leatherette in Black, Graphite grey, Savanna (tan), Metropole blue, Space grey. Special colours: Nephrite green, Boxster red
Cabriolet roof colours
Black, Classic grey, Dark blue, Chestnut

1998
External body colours
Black, Guards red, Pastel yellow, Glacier white, Ocean blue metallic, Zenith blue metallic, Arena red metallic, Arctic silver metallic, Ocean jade metallic, Black metallic, Mirage metallic, Vesuvio grey metallic
Interiors
Leather/leatherette in Black, Graphite grey, Savanna (tan), Metropole blue, Space grey. Special colours: Nephrite green, Boxster red.
Cabriolet roof colours
Black, Classic grey, Dark blue, Chestnut

1999
External body colours
Black, Guards Red, Pastel yellow, Glacier White, Ocean Blue metallic, Zenith Blue metallic, Arena Red metallic, Arctic Silver metallic, Ocean Jade metallic, Black metallic, Mirage metallic, Vesuvio Grey metallic
Special order colours
Wimbledon green metallic, Forest green metallic, Slate grey metallic, Cobalt Blue metallic, Midnight blue metallic (Cabriolet only), Viola metallic, Dark blue, Polar silver metallic, Iris blue metallic, Speed yellow, non-metallic colour to sample, Metallic colour to sample
Interiors
Leather/leatherette in Black, Graphite grey, Savanna (tan), Metropole blue, Space grey. Special colours: Nephrite green and Boxster red
Cabriolet roof colours
Black, Classic Grey, Dark Blue, Chestnut

2000
External body colours
Black, Basalt black metallic, Biarritz white, Arctic silver metallic, Meridian metallic, Seal grey metallic, Speed yellow, Zanzibar red metallic (GT3/Turbo only), Guards red, Orient red metallic, Rainforest green metallic , Lapis blue metallic
Special order colours
Wimbledon green metallic, Forest green metallic, Slate grey metallic, Cobalt Blue metallic, Midnight blue metallic, Viola metallic, Dark blue, Polar silver metallic, Iris blue metallic, Violet chrome metallic (Millennium only), metallic and non-metallic colours to sample,
Interiors
Black, Graphite grey, Savanna, Metropole blue, Nephrite green, Boxter red (special order), Cinnamon brown (special order), Dark grey (natural leather option), Natural brown (natural leather option), Leather to customer colour match
Cabriolet roof colours
Graphite grey, Metropole blue, Black

2001
External body colours
Black metallic, Biarritz white, Arctic silver metallic, Meridian metalic, Seal grey metallic, Speed yellow, Zanzibar red metallic, Guards red, Orient red metallic, Rainforest green metallic, Lapis blue metallic

Special order colours

Wimbledon green metallic, Forest green metallic, Slate grey metallic, Cobalt blue metallic, Midnight blue metallic, Viola metallic, Dark blue, Polar silver metallic, Metallic and non-metallic colour to sample

Interiors

Black, Graphite grey, Savanna, Metropole blue, Nephrite green, Boxster red (special order), Cinnamon brown (special order), Dark grey (natural leather option), Natural brown (natural leather option), Leather to customer colour match

Cabriolet roof colours

Graphite grey, Metropole blue, Black

2002
External body colours

Black, Basalt black metallic, Carrara white, Arctic silver metallic, Meridian metallic, Seal grey metallic, Speed yellow, Zanzibar red metallic, Guards red, Orient red metallic, Rainforest green metallic, Lapis blue metallic

Special order colours

Forest green metallic, Slate grey metallic, Cobalt blue metallic, Midnight blue metallic, Polar silver metallic, metallic and non-metallic colour to sample.

Interiors

Black, Graphite grey, Savanna, Metropole blue, Nephrite green, Boxster red (special order), Cinnamon brown (special order), Dark grey and natural brown (natural leather options), Leather to customer colour match

Cabriolet roof colours

Graphite grey, Metropole blue, Black

2003
External body colours

Black, Carrara white, Guards red, Speed yellow, Orient red metallic, Meridian metallic, Lagoongreen metallic, Midnight blue metallic, Lapis blue metallic, Arctic silver metallic, Seal grey metallic, Basalt black metallic

Special order colours

Forest green metallic, Cobalt blue metallic, Polar silver metallic, Slate grey metallic, Zanzibar red metallic

Interiors

Leather for steering wheel rim, door handle front, glovebox, side airbag covers, storage bin lid, gearlever, handbrake, seat centre, lateral supports and head restraint. Sun visors are in leatherette (grained vinyl), with metal fittings in soft touch paint.

Black, Graphite grey, Savanna, Metropole blue, Nephrite green, Boxster red (special order), Cinnamon brown (special order), Dark grey and Natural brown (natural leather options), leather to customer colour match

Cabriolet roof colours

Graphite grey, Metropole blue, Black

2004
External body colours

Black, Carrara white, Guards red, Speed yellow, Carmon red metallic (not GT2 or GT3), Atlas grey metallic (not GT2 or GT3), Midnight blue metallic, Dark teal metallic (N. America), Lapis blue metallic, Arctic silver metallic, Seal grey metallic, Basalt black metallic

Special order colours

Forest green metallic, Cobalt blue metallic, Polar silver metallic, Slate grey metallic, Meridian metallic

Interiors

Black, Graphite grey, Savanna, Metropole blue, Nephrite green, Boxster red (special order), Cinnamon brown (special order), Dark grey (natural leather option), Natural brown (natural leather option), Leather to customer colour match

Cabriolet roof colours

Graphite Grey, Metropole Blue, Black

Options

In terms of residual value, 996's are fairly specification sensitive, with used prices influenced by whether certain key options fitted (namely 18-inch wheels, sunroof, climate control, leather, sat-nav, etc.). This list gives the most popular options and their VIL codes

Exterior

Litronic headlamps (self-level w/wash) - 601

Headlight cleaning system - 288

Bi Xenon Lights (self-level w/wash) - P74

Deletion of model designation - 498

Windscreen with green top tint - 567

Rear wiper - 425

Park assist - 635

Autodimming mirror/rain sensor - P11

Electric Tilt slide Sunroof - 650

Wind deflector (Cab) - 551

Hard top Cabriolet - XC3

Cup Aerokit (pre-facelift cars) - XAA

Carrera 4S aerokit - Y75

Turbo Aerokit - XAF

Carrera aero kit - XAE

Carrera rear spoiler only - XAG

Side skirts only- X76

GT rear side trims - XAD

Roof transport system - 549

Engine and chassis

Sports exhaust - XLF

Stainless steel tail pipes - X54

Performance Power Kit (pre-facelift 320bhp) - X51

Powerkit (facelift 345bhp) - X51

Powerkit (Turbo) - X50

Tiptronic S - 249

Traction control and ABD - 222 and 224

Porsche Stability Management (PSM) - 476

Sports Chassis (-10mm) - 030

Sports chassis (-30mm) - X74

Sports chassis on Turbo (-20mm) - X73

18" Carrera wheels - 411

18" Turbo-look 1 wheels - 413 (polished - 414)

18" SportClassic 2 wheels - XRB

18" SportsDesign wheels - XRL

18" Sport Techno

18" Turbo-look 2

Wider Wheels (with 285/30ZR tyres at rear) - XRM

5-mm spacers front/rear - XRP

17-mm spacers on rear axle - XRN

Coloured wheel centres - 446

Painted wheels - XD9

Interior

Instrument dials in interior colour - X45

Cruise Control - 454

On-Board Computer - 659

Full Memory Electric seats - P15

Heated seats - P14

Lumber Support: left - 586, right - 513 (only P15)

Lowered front seats - XSU

Soft Ruffled Leather seats - 982

Sports seats - P89

Sports seat backs in leather - XSB

Sports seat backs in exterior colour - XSA

Bucket seat: left - XSE; right - XSF

Safety roll-over bar - XSL

Colour s/belts: XSX (red), XSY (yellow), XSW (blue)

Rear section of centre console in body colour - XME

Footwell lighting/central switch - XX2

Full Leather Interior - L1 (standard in UK)

Leather interior in natural leather - X99

Porsche crest embossed in head rest - XSC

Lid of storage compartment with logo - CUV

Interior in natural leather - X99

Leather package small - E74

Leather package large - E70

Three spoke leather sports steering wheel - XPA

Four spoke steering wheel in leather - X26

Steering column in leather - XNS

PCM handset in leather - XEA

Front section of centre console leather - XMF

Rear section of centre console in leather - XMZ

Rooflining in leather - XMA

Sun visors in leather - XMP

Interior light cover in leather - XZD

Inner sill in leather - XTG

Seat controls in leather - XSD

Floor Mats - XX1

Burr Maple package small - (light) E75 (dark) E76

Burr Maple package large - (light) E71 (dark) E72

Burr Maple gearlever/hbrake - (light) Y07 (dark) Y08

Burr Maple tiptronic/hbrake - (light) Y62 (dark) Y63

Burr Maple centre console - (light) XML (dark) XNB

Carbon package small - E77

Carbon package large - E73

3-spoke sports steering wheel with carbon - XPD

Gear lever and handbrake in carbon - Y05

Tiptronic lever and handbrake in carbon - Y61

Rear section of centre console in carbon - XMJ

Door entry guards in carbon - X69

Arctic silver package small - E61

Arctic silver package large - E78

Rear of the centre console in Arctic Silver - XJB

Instrument surround in Arctic Silver - XKX

Aluminium/stainless steel/chrome package - Y29

Aluminium coloured instrument dials - X71

Gear lever and handbrake in aluminium - Y06

Tiptronic lever and handbrake in aluminium - Y23

Tiptronic lever with aluminium inlay & leather - XY5

Door entry guards in stainless steel - X70

Porsche CDR-22 CD radio - 695

Porsche CDR-32 CD radio - 698

Porsche MDR-32 MiniDisc radio - 699

CDC-3 CD autochanger - 692

Porsche Sound Package - 490

Porsche DSP Digital Sound Processing - P49

Bose sound system (analogue) - 680

Porsche Communication Management - 662 PCM2

PCM handset - 663

Porsche Exclusive

The Porsche Exclusive selection introduces an additional and very comprehensive list of custom options that can be specified at the time of order and are fitted at the factory before delivery. These options include full bodykits, performance upgrades, In-Car Entertainment packages and alternative trim materials (such as carbonfibre and maple wood finishes).

The full Porsche Exclusive options list is too extensive to show here

In the US there is also a range of upgrade packs that include a number of options under one code.

For example consider the TECHNICS package:

P03 – this includes Litronic lights with washer system, OBC, uprated hi-fi system with CD radio and CD shelf, plus the wind deflector for the Cabriolet.

Country codes

Porsche builds cars for many different markets. With high demand for the 996 series, cars that were originally built for other countries are often imported outside the receiving country's official network. However, the standard specification for one country may not be the same as another and key options can be omitted. Porsche give each car a destination country code and it is easy to identify this. The best residual prices will always be achieved by cars with the same country code as where you live.

We have listed some of the main country codes below.

C00 Germany, C02 Rest of USA, C03 California, C05 France, C07 Italy, C08 Japan (LHD), C09 Sweden, C10 Switzerland, C11 Austria, C12 Denmark, C13 Finland, C15 Hong Kong, C16 GB, C17 British service personnel stationed in Germany, C18 Japan (RHD), C19 Luxemburg, C20 Holland, C21 Norway, C22 Belgium, C23 Australia, C24 New Zealand, C26 South Africa, C27 Spain, C28 Greece, C36 Canada, C98 Non-specific RHD

Buying a used 996

There are some basic rules that apply to buying any used car. Most importantly, don't buy on impulse. If you like a car, but the checking bores you, get an expert to look at it. It could save you thousands on either repair bills or when you come to sell it. If you have to put a holding deposit on the car, keep it as small as possible. Many dealers will refuse to refund a deposit if you change your mind.

996s are used everyday for business and fun, rather than as a third car kept only for weekends. Consequently, the odometer readings (the distance covered) can easily average 10-12,000 miles (16-20,000km) a year. That said, specialist trackday cars such as the GT3 often have lower than typical odometer readings.

The most important aspect of buying the car is its condition, but close behind is proof of origin and a water-tight service history.

This section will go into greater detail on the areas of the car that must be checked before purchase, starting with that all-important documentation.

Documentation

If the car hasn't got a full service history, the owner hasn't got the registration documents, the car appears too cheap or you have any concerns on the points we will discuss below, walk away.

On page 4 of the Guarantee and Maintenance Book you will find the delivery date and the stamp of the supplying OPC. Next to this is the Vehicle Identification Label (VIL).

The VIL carries the car's Vehicle Identification Number (VIN or chassis number), engine and transmission type, paint and interior code, together with a listing of the factory options (listed first is the important country code) fitted to the car. Another identical label is located under the front compartment bonnet. When these labels are missing, then the origins of the car must be verified separately.

The specification of the country code affects its resale value and your peace of mind. Many Official Porsche Centres (OPCs) won't trade in cars that do not carry the correct country code.

It is not unusual to find grey-import cars in your own country. For example, you may find 'C98' cars in Britain, particularly from the period 1999 to 2001, when prices in mainland Europe were lower.

Although many sellers claim to have upgraded these cars to full GB specification, it is sometimes hard to be sure. You may end up without a top tinted screen or the correct stereo, or you may find that air conditioning or the full leather interior is missing. There are also insurance issues attached to cars that do not match the correct specification for your country.

Cars that have the correct country code (e.g. C16 UK, C02/03 US etc) but have been supplied outside the official in-country network, are still desirable, but worth slightly less than official cars. There are other service and warranty implications applicable to a car bought outside the official network of your home country.

The car's VIN is stamped on to the metal plate at the foot of the windscreen's left side and appears on a non-removable label by driver's door catch.

The front of the service book may also have the names and addresses of

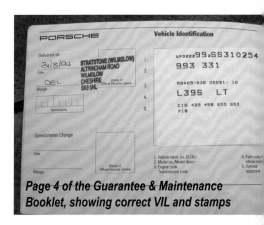

Page 4 of the Guarantee & Maintenance Booklet, showing correct VIL and stamps

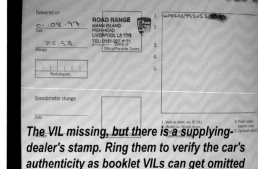

The VIL missing, but there is a supplying-dealer's stamp. Ring them to verify the car's authenticity as booklet VILs can get omitted

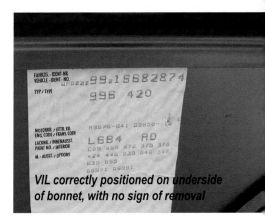

VIL correctly positioned on underside of bonnet, with no sign of removal

the previous owners listed. The previous owner's address information may also be shown on the registration document (In the UK, called the V5). It can be well worth a call, especially if you have doubts about the car's past.

The book will also include a record of the service history, the brake fluid change intervals and the annual authorisations for the 10 year body warranty against rust perforation. The service record may have the odd stamp missing, but the ideal is an unbroken run, with stamps every year (depending on distance covered).

Official Porsche Centres (OPC) are generally very good at picking up all faults in a car during a routine service (and will note them on the invoice).

If the owner has a neat stack of paperwork relating to the car, this is usually the sign of an enthusiast who has looked after it. If they are available, check the service invoices (and any annual roadworthiness check documents – MoTs in the UK) against the service book stamps, dates and distances recorded, noting any anomalies.

Many owners look for better value than the official network can offer and it is not unusual to find a recognised specialist has taken over the servicing after about 3-4 years, 40,000 miles, or when the mechanical warranties expire. It is important to say that the best independents have all the correct diagnostic equipment and can look after a 996 as well as any OPC. The only downside to this cheaper servicing option is that it can compromise the car's 10 year warranty against rust perforation. For clarification on this, we advise you talk to your nearest OPC before you buy a car. If you make this call, you can also ask if they can trace the original build/order sheet for the car, that will prove it is in-country supplied, this should also be available via Porsche customer services using the cars VIN.

But whether an OPC or an independent has looked after the car, call them to get a clearer picture on the car's history.

Cars that haven't been well looked after (or serviced by poorly-equipped independents) may have hidden problems. This particularly applies to the electronics and the associated

The chassis number label is on the driver's door catch pillar

The paint code label is on the side wall of the front compar

911 Carrera 4 coupé

engine management software.

It goes without saying that unpleasant bills are likely to be left out of the document pack, so this search shouldn't replace a thorough inspection of the car itself. Note also that any paperwork can be faked, so look out for photocopied documents, service books that do not have the VIL at the front or non-authentic service stamps.

Finally, there is also a market for left-hand drive (LHD) cars in certain right-hand drive markets (for instance, in the UK). You pay less for LHD, but you also get less on resale. If the position of the steering wheel doesn't bother you, these cars usually offer much better value for money. But such cars are generally harder to sell.

Bodyshell

Generally the 996 is very hard wearing inside and out, so if it's been properly looked after it should look clean and tidy even if it has high miles. Having said this the darker colours do seem to be more prone to showing the scratches and swirls that a car's paint work picks up along the way, but a good cutting wax (in the right hands) can probably sort this.

As we have already discussed, the 996 has a fully galvanised bodyshell and the best cars will have an intact 10 year official warranty against rust perforation (see the Guarantee and Maintenance Book).

The front of the car is prone to stone chips (as are the fronts of the rear wings or fenders and the exterior mirrors). If the car has no chips on the front and has a typical mileage, then it is possible that it has had a cosmetic repaint in the affected areas. If the quality is good, the only issue is whether the

10-year paintwork warranty is still valid, but you should also ensure it hasn't been in an accident.

Excessive stone chipping or pitting on a low mileage car be suspicious, it could be a sign of a heavily used trackday car (with all the extra wear and tear that brings) or that the mileage may be higher than declared.

At the front end check for front spoiler and underbody damage. It is very easy to ground a 996 (particularly a Turbo or a GT3) and the repair bill can be significant.

High value, prestige cars like the 996 are rarely written off so check very carefully for any signs of past accident damage. The simple tell-tale signs are paint overspray and poorly refitted trim (particularly fasteners missing). Check each panel for misalignment (doors, front and rear lids and trim parts), paint imperfections and any unusual marks or dents. The front and rear bumpers are made to withstand low speed parking bumps, but if the paintwork is cracked or crazed, it may indicate more serious damage.

Most importantly, look at the underbody (using a safe lifting method if possible), wheelarches and inside the front and rear compartments. Remove the front compartment carpet moulding and check for signs of damage or repair to the chassis longitudinals at each side (a missing paint code sticker, for instance), the front wall and the floor. In the engine bay, look for evidence of repair work that might include differences from side to side, poor welding or new paint.

If you are looking at a Cabriolet be sure to check the roof material carefully inside and out for rips and tears. On the test drive, wind noise shouldn't be an issue. If the roof is

Check the front of the car carefully for misalignment and damage. Chipping here is common, crazing of the paint (from collisions) isn't

The inside of the front compartment with the carpet removed. Note the stove-in frontal area, indicating accident damage

The front underbody is very vulnerable to damage from kerb contact. This damage repair suggests a heavier collision

Check the front underbody for kerbing scrapes or evidence of harder shunts. This is how it should look

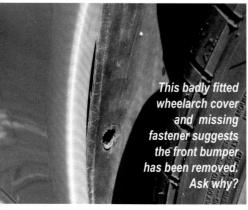

This badly fitted wheelarch cover and missing fastener suggests the front bumper has been removed. Ask why?

The flexible splitter on the front of the Turbo is very prone to accidental damage

noisy, adjustments may be required.

Check the plastic rear window (on pre-2002 models) for cracks, splits and imperfections. The rear window is a weak point and can split if raised and lowered in particularly cold weather (Porsche have advised not less than 10C for the Boxster's similar item). To replace the window normally means replacing the whole roof.

Pre-2000 models were fitted with door catches that bolted directly to the body. There have been instances of rust developing under these catches. The fix (on later models) was to fit a plastic gasket between the catch and the body. Cars that developed this problem may have been rectified under the 10-year body warranty, but it is worth checking. If you find more serious rust (anywhere on the body) it will suggest poor accident damage repair.

Metallic paint is standard in many markets with the most popular colour being silver, followed by the darker shades of grey, blues and blacks (like Lapis, Cobalt, Midnight, Basalt etc). The reds, whites and yellows aren't the current top sellers!

The colour will affect the value of the car quite significantly. You don't normally get much colour choice when it comes to buying a used car (and factors like condition, documentation, etc are more important). But a 996 in a popular colour will be more desirable and easier to sell. The other side of this is that cars in the less popular colours can represent better value.

Equipment and accessories

To save frustration after you have bought the car, check that everything works. First, check all the warning lights come on as the ignition is turned and that these extinguish once the car is started.

Establish that the battery is no more than 4 years old. Getting into the 996 without undue hassle is completely dependent on having a good battery. If this goes flat, then the electronic release to the front compartment (where it is housed) won't work and special jumper leads will be required. This will be a particular problem on cars that have not been used very much.

Check all the electrical accessories work as they should, including the sunroof (open and tilt functions), exterior mirrors (plus their heating), seat adjustment, windows (including the one-touch operation), wash/wipe, headlamp washers (if fitted) and the cigarette lighter. It is important the lighter socket works, so that you can power portable accessories. Don't forget to operate the engine bay and front compartment releases, by the side of the driver's seat. On 2001 models, the front compartment could be opened remotely from the key fob.

The climate control is very efficient on the 996. Cycle the system through high and low settings and check the heater works at all fan speeds. There shouldn't be any unusual noises. If the cooling performance feels poor (particularly on an older car) then the air conditioner system may need recharging. The front-mounted condenser may cause water droplets to drip from under the front of the car. This is normal, and doesn't mean you have problems or leaking radiators, (although you must always check coolant level to be sure!).

Turn on all the lights (including fog, by pulling out light switch) and hazard flashers. Walk around the car to check these all are

Check all the accessories work!

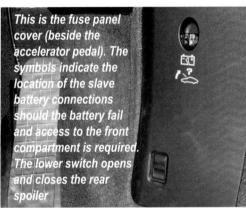

This is the fuse panel cover (beside the accelerator pedal). The symbols indicate the location of the slave battery connections should the battery fail and access to the front compartment is required. The lower switch opens and closes the rear spoiler

The compartment release levers for the pre-2001 models

The Targa body style offers an electrically-operated panoramic sunroof and this useful opening rear tailgate

Be wary of after-market installed ICE systems. This is the factory Bose speaker installation

working. Operate the rear spoiler (you can manually raise this while the car is stationary by pressing a button on the fuse panel (or the dash on the Turbo)).

If the car has a factory-fitted Porsche CR22 or 32 radio/CD in-car entertainment system and perhaps a factory-fitted immobiliser, then you can usually assume the wiring is as it should be. But check it all works.

The factory-fitted alarm system should close all windows and the sunroof if you press and hold down the key fob button. If the car has stood for a while and the remote won't open the car, the alarm has gone into "sleep mode" (for extra security). Simply unlock the door with the key (this wakes the alarm from sleep mode), use the remote to turn the alarm off, then open the door. If you open the door straight away the alarm will go off (and have earplugs ready!).

What can ruin a good car are poorly fitted after-market ICE or immobiliser/alarm systems. Look under the dash and the adjacent fuse panel for signs of rats' nest wiring. Poor electrics can destroy the car's reliability.

Visually check the headlight assemblies for signs of chips or cracking. They are very tough but are one piece units. If they need to be replaced you cannot just buy the outer covers.

Be wary of any after-market modifications. While a sports exhaust and upgraded induction system may be fine (if you like the throatier noise!), anything else (like more complex engine modifications) could cause headaches. This is not only a reliability issue. Such unofficial modifications may invalidate any warranties. Even if it's only a sports exhaust, then be sure to check that the owner still has his original system. Come resale time, an OPC will not buy a car with a non-approved system fitted unless the original is available to refit.

Interior

The new generation Porsches use a lot of plastic 'snap-fit' fasteners for the interior trim. These don't like being used more than once or twice and on the early cars (1997-98) they seem to age rapidly and rattle. 996s are prone to the odd interior trim noise. This can drive you nuts, until it suddenly goes as quickly as it came! Trim noise is usually not anything serious but it can indicate that the car has been taken apart for repairs.

A 2001 model with 3-position seat memory facility

The front compartment on the 2001-onwards models could be opened from the key fob (rear button)

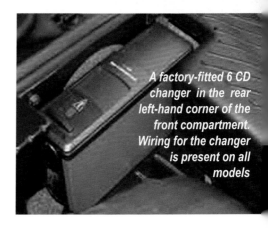

A factory-fitted 6 CD changer in the rear left-hand corner of the front compartment. Wiring for the changer is present on all models

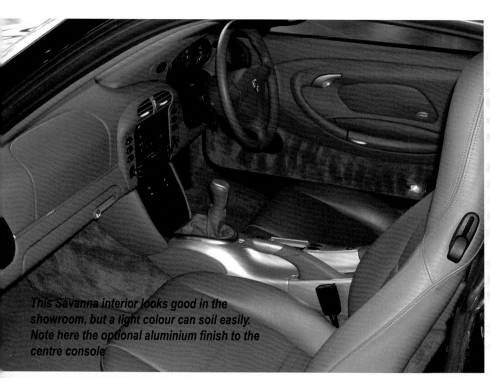

This Savanna interior looks good in the showroom, but a light colour can soil easily. Note here the optional aluminium finish to the centre console

The rear seat backs fold flat to form a useful storage area

Generally, the 996 interior is fairly robust. Ideally, the interior should be clean and unmarked with no unpleasant odours (particularly stale smoke). Check the front and rear seats, the carpeting and the headlining for any nicks or tears. The front of the seat squab and the outer bolster can get scuffed with heavy use.

Earlier cars (pre-2001) had long, chrome-look bonnet and boot releases next to the drivers door sill. These tend to get kicked or scuffed as you get in and out the car, so it's not unusual for them to get scuffed and a little tatty.

Be sure to touch the carpets (including that on the lower doors) to check for dampness. Look for other signs that water is getting into the cabin, particularly on Cabriolets.

In the front compartment, the pre-formed carpet is easily marked and the hard plastics used also tend to get marked with age.

The darker, more subdued shades are the popular colours for the interior. Top of the list is black, with Metropole Blue also very popular. The more lively colours include Savannah (a caramel shade), Graphite Grey and Boxster Red (an extra cost terracotta shade). The Boxster Red can go orange with time, while the Caramel and grey can show grime and marks easily. A wild card is Nephrite green, which with a matching exterior colour is certainly different.

Engine

A very small percentage of the early cars (1997-99) have been affected by serious engine failures. These failures have included porous crankcases causing the coolant and oil to mix (with inevitable results), cracked cylinder liners, failed intermediate shaft

Tatty carpets let the car down. However, this right heel mark demonstrates the value of overcarpets

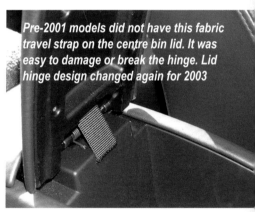

Pre-2001 models did not have this fabric travel strap on the centre bin lid. It was easy to damage or break the hinge. Lid hinge design changed again for 2003

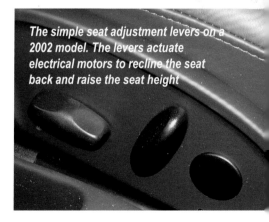

The simple seat adjustment levers on a 2002 model. The levers actuate electrical motors to recline the seat back and raise the seat height

bearings and poor oil circulation during hard cornering. It is believed most of these issues were rectified by Porsche under the original warranties, but such tales point to the fact that serious failures still can and do occur. If you want more up-to-date information, we suggest you tap into the various internet focus groups on the 996. Oil surge was not an issue on the Turbo or the GT3 as these high performance models used an engine block derived from the racing GT1.

A more mainstream problem for the water-cooled 996 engine concerns the rear main oil seal, which has a tendency to 'sweat' oil (particularly when the thin 0W/40 Mobil 1 engine oil is used). The leaks are often minor (depositing a film of oil on the rear of the crankcase over time), but are still undesirable on an expensive, prestige sports car.

Although the oil seal is not expensive itself, the labour involved with fitting one is! If you are buying an early car, ensure that it has Porsche's modified rear main oil seal fitted (check the bills or talk to the OPC). Be sure to check the parking area floor for tell tale spots of oil and once the engine is warmed up, note any strong oil smells from the engine area. Ideally, get the car on a garage ramp and look for signs of a persistent oil leak (as defined above).

Otherwise, the 996 has been very reliable (despite the 'they don't build them like they used to' claims). Nevertheless, regular maintenance is crucial, so be concerned if the car you are looking at hasn't been properly serviced (the recommended interval is yearly or 12,000 miles/20,000km whichever is sooner). For those cars that are infrequently used, the annual oil change can still be worthwhile as in certain climates the oil can become water-saturated and actually

The water-cooled 6-cylinder engine has, in general, been very reliable. Nevertheless, there have been issues

increase the chances of internal corrosion.

Checking the oil has never been easier on all but the GTs and the Turbo (which require the engine to be warmed up and running). You put the key into the ignition, turn it (don't start the car unless it's a GT or the Turbo) and watch the oil measure appear in the display below the rev counter.

The 996 can use more oil than a regular family saloon (for instance). While this isn't anything to worry about, it does mean you need to keep a regular check on levels. Some owners get caught out, so if the car's oil level is low, be wary. It is also still worth checking the dipstick, (but note that the Turbo doesn't have one) to see the quality and colour of the oil. If it is jet black, then it is probably well overdue for a service. If there is excessive creaming in the oil filler cap, or signs of water droplets on the dipstick, then there could be oil/water mixing problems or be a sign of an infrequently used car.

The coolant should be at the maximum level. If it isn't, ask the owner if he has topped up the level recently and take a look around the rest of the coolant circuit to check for leaks. It is possible (although unlikely) for the front mounted radiators to get damaged by road debris.

On start up, the engine can make a sound like dried peas in a can for a few seconds. This is nothing as long as the engine settles down afterwards. The hydraulic valve play adjusters can empty of oil if the car stands for any length of time. They can make a noise before they fill with oil. Once the engine is warmed through, the oil pressure should be stable and there should be no exhaust smoke, hesitation or misfiring detectable at any revolutions.

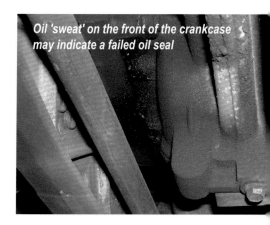

Oil 'sweat' on the front of the crankcase may indicate a failed oil seal

Oil leaks from the lower camshaft covers are a perennial flat-6 issue

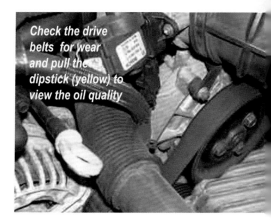

Check the drive belts for wear and pull the dipstick (yellow) to view the oil quality

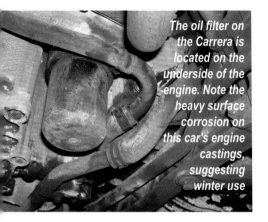

The oil filter on the Carrera is located on the underside of the engine. Note the heavy surface corrosion on this car's engine castings, suggesting winter use

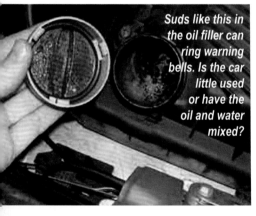

Suds like this in the oil filler can ring warning bells. Is the car little used or have the oil and water mixed?

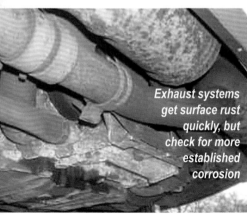

Exhaust systems get surface rust quickly, but check for more established corrosion

Transmission

The 6-speed manual gearbox can be rather notchy when cold, but should be fast and slick once the oil is warm.

There should be no evidence of graunching or baulking as the gear is selected. If there is there could be a problem with the synchromesh. The cable-operated gearshift has proven to be very reliable. Some cars may have after-market short-shift kits that significantly improve the 'connected' feel of the lever to the gearbox, but the trade-off is that you feel far more of the car's natural vibrations.

Some early cars also seemed to suffer from potentially fragile clutches and although this should have been corrected by now, it is still an area that needs checking carefully. Listen for clutch rattle when the engine is idling (this will disappear when you put your foot on the clutch). Check for clutch slip or judder, particularly in reverse or on a hill start. The clutch should not slip when accelerating hard from low speed in second gear. The clutch pedal action should not be heavy.

In normal use (a mix of urban and touring) a sympathetically-driven clutch should last at least 50,000miles (80,000km) before replacement becomes due.

The Porsche automatic option is called Tiptronic S. Tiptronic offers both full automatic and clutchless manual shift modes and has a good reputation in the marketplace.

It is important to check all the operating modes, including the steering wheel button operation (the 'S' in Tiptronic S). When you test drive the car, operate it in both full automatic and manual shift positions, taking time to use both the lever and buttons to upshift and downshift. Afterwards, take a look

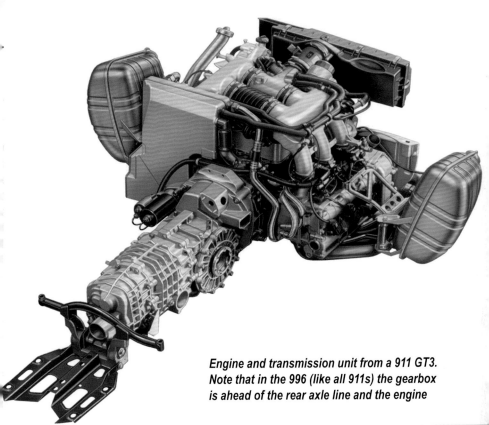

*Engine and transmission unit from a 911 GT3.
Note that in the 996 (like all 911s) the gearbox
is ahead of the rear axle line and the engine*

under the car to ensure there are no obvious leaks from the transmission housing.

Finally, if the car can be raised safely (not using its own jack, but either on a professional ramp or with a heavy duty hydraulic jack, supplemented with the correct type of stands), check the condition of the driveshaft rubber boots for splits.

You will probably only be able to see the outer items, but a split driveshaft boot can allow debris into the constant velocity joint, which is often only detected (too late) by hearing a knocking sound under acceleration or after lifting the accelerator. This last point re-emphasises the benefits of having the car checked over by a Porsche specialist with the right equipment. Such checks are definitely money well spent.

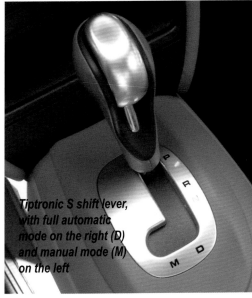

*Tiptronic S shift lever,
with full automatic
mode on the right (D)
and manual mode (M)
on the left*

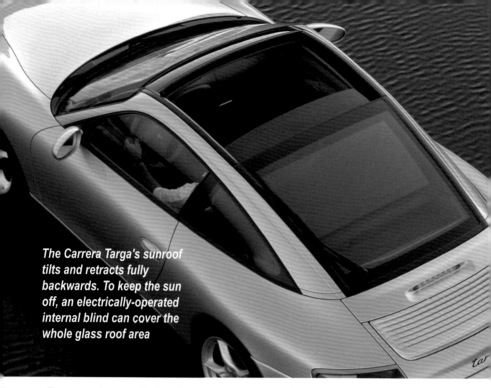

The Carrera Targa's sunroof tilts and retracts fully backwards. To keep the sun off, an electrically-operated internal blind can cover the whole glass roof area

Suspension and steering

You are unlikely to find any issues with the suspension (as this is very robust) unless there has been accident damage or the car is high mileage.

Check for leaks from the struts and damage to the lower control arms (from grounding). On older cars, lift the wheels off the ground and check for worn anti-roll bar and steering rack bushes. With high mileage cars it is also worth listening out for a whining noise that could indicate worn wheel bearings. If possible, with the car off the ground, check the boots on the steering rack are not leaking and that those on the drive shafts are not split.

One of the more common issues is misaligned geometry, the 996 has a comprehensive wheel alignment system that needs to be accurately set to ensure the car is handling correctly. This is particularly

relevant with all that engine weight slung out over the rear axle. Badly kerbing the wheels or hitting a large hole can knock the geometry out of alignment and affect the car's handling. Having this geometry reset doesn't come cheap.

Even though it is a sports car, the 996 should have a compliant but very confident ride. It should feel extremely stable and accurately follow your steering inputs. Traction under full throttle shouldn't be an issue with all that weight over the rear wheels.

The new generation 996 is an extremely easy car to drive at normal speeds and you shouldn't have to feel you are adapting to any quirks in its character.

Only under extreme cornering loads (if the car is on standard suspension) should you notice a degree of body roll, accompanied by some diagonal pitching. At this level of

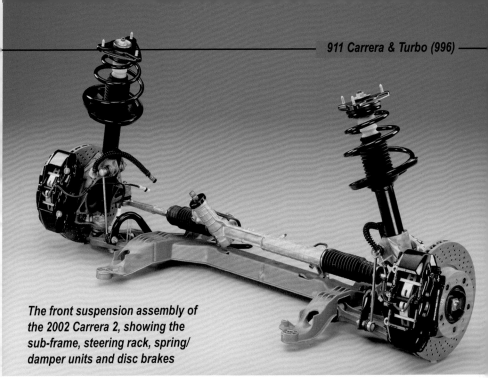

The front suspension assembly of the 2002 Carrera 2, showing the sub-frame, steering rack, spring/damper units and disc brakes

The rear suspension assembly of the Carrera 2 shows the rear subframe and drive shafts

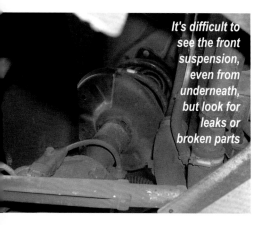

It's difficult to see the front suspension, even from underneath, but look for leaks or broken parts

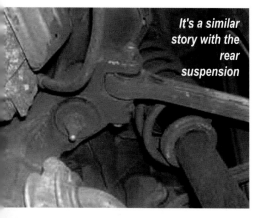

It's a similar story with the rear suspension

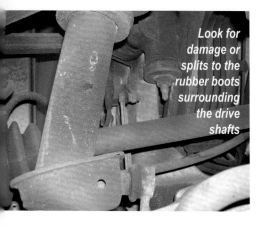

Look for damage or splits to the rubber boots surrounding the drive shafts

commitment the car can also understeer.

If you notice anything that feels odd at normal speeds, or if there is a tendency to wander on unrutted roads, then there's probably something wrong.

If the car has the 10mm lowered suspension (standard on the C4S and Turbo) then you should experience virtually zero body roll, pitching or understeer – even at the limit. The trade-off is that the ride will be harsher than standard. If you are test-driving a car with the 30mm lowered set (or even the recommended 10mm lowered) be sure to find a bumpy road to see if you can live with the ride quality on a daily basis!

Brakes, wheels and tyres

Unscrupulous dealers will remove expensive 18-inch optional wheels and fit the regular 17-inch items. Inexperienced buyers won't know the difference, but the desirability of the car is influenced strongly by the wheels. If a car comes with the 18-inch wheels listed in the options (see the list starting on page 36) and they are not on the car, ask why. Check with the owner as to whether the wheels are original Porsche items or cheaper after-market items.

Check each alloy wheel for marks and scuffs, either from poorly fitted tyres or as a result of wheel refurbishment.

Poorly refurbished wheels are identified by badly-prepared alloy surfaces, paint and lacquer and differing colour and textures. If the wheels are not refurbished correctly, the new finish will come off within a few months.

The wheels should have one locking wheelnut per wheel, but check that the correct key socket is in the toolkit. If that

The Carrera's major mechanical units comprise the engine, transmission and suspension

Rusty brake discs can deliver poor brake performance

This brake disc is showing heavy tramlining (grooving) between the drillings

is lost, the wheels can only be removed by an official Porsche dealer. But don't panic, replacements are available!

All 996s are fitted with Porsche approved N-rated tyres from new; these have special compounds designed to suit the handling characteristics of the car. Some owners aren't aware of this and fit non-approved tyres – sometimes mixing N- and non N-rated tyres (often this is because the rears wear faster than the fronts). This practice, and fitting different makes of tyre on each axle, can be dangerous.

The rating (e.g. N2 etc.) will be stamped on the sidewall of the tyre. For similar reasons, 996s should only be fitted with premium brand tyres, typically Michelin, Pirelli or

Continental. Other makes are approved by Porsche for aftermarket fitting, and your local Porsche specialist will be able to advise you on this.

Use a tyre tread meter to measure the depth of tread, across the full width of the tyre. The European Union-approved legal limit is 1.6mm minimum.

The 996 uses relatively high tyre pressures (2.5bar or 36psi front and 3.0bar or 44psi rear) and combined with the wheel's camber and toe settings, can cause the tyres to wear more in the middle or inner edges.

If the tyres aren't N-rated or are getting low on tread, build the price of changing them in to your buying price.

The performance of the brakes is simply awesome, but on your test drive you may be taken by surprise when you first press the middle pedal and find you aren't stopping fast enough! This is normal. They sometimes need a firm push on the first application.

Once warmed up, the car will feel like it will stand on its nose when you brake hard and as importantly, the ABS system will only cut in when it's needed. But if the car pulls continually to one side then they may need work. The usual reasons are either worn pads or rusty discs. Rust can be caused by lack of use or pressure washing and then leaving the brakes to air dry!

Be sure to check the brake discs visually for signs of rusting as well as wear. Check the drill holes in the discs, as these become blocked over time and this increases the heat build up in the brakes.

One of the very few less durable areas of the GT3 are its brakes. Although fine for road use, it is generally felt that they aren't up to the higher demands placed on them by

2002-model 18-inch Carrera wheel

Damage to the wheelrim from kerb contact

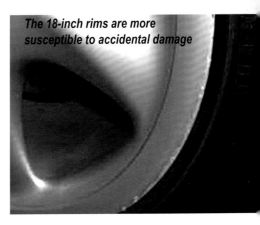
The 18-inch rims are more susceptible to accidental damage

10-spoke 17-inch Carrera II wheel used from the start of the 2002 model year (the 'facelift' cars)

18-inch Turbo-look 2 wheel on Carrera

5-spoke 17-inch wheel on a Carrera 4

regular high speed track work. If you suspect a car has been used for track work, check the condition of the brakes carefully and establish whether any upgrades have been fitted (for instance harder road/race pads and iimproved cooling ducts at the front).

While certain brake upgrades can be great on track, they can compromise the road usability. Harder pads for instance, can squeal loudly, wear the discs faster and require more heat to make them work properly.

Certain enthusiast owners will modify or change the suspension, tyres or engine performance. While this may be fine if you too are looking to get maximum performance on track, it will compromise the cars on road performance and most importantly, its resale value. Most buyers prefer cars that are in their original specification.

Finally, don't forget to take out the toolkit and unroll it, look at the jack and the emergency wheel. 996s use a slender pre-inflated emergency wheel and so do not need a compressor. And unfortunately for the GT drivers, Porsche do not even provide the emergency wheel!

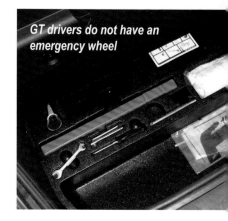

GT drivers do not have an emergency wheel

*Ceramic brake disc and
yellow 6-piston caliper*

*The standard toolkit, jack and
emergency wheel is in the front
compartment.*

Coolant check
Check the coolant in the header tank is clear and
correct level. Any milkiness should be investigated f

What to look for — at a glance

Interior
Check bonnet and boot release as
these are prone to damage. Check seat
sides for scuffing and flip seats forward to
check their backs for damage. Gear levers
and door trims can be damaged by ring
wearers. Check the centre console bin lid
for breakage

Electrical
Ensure all the warning lights illuminate
as the ignition is turned on and that they
extinguish once the car has started. Check
the windows, mirrors, wipers, indicators,
lights, stereo and rear spoiler all work.

Check VIN numbers
You will find the Vehicle Identification
Number (chassis number) stamped
into a plate on the passenger-side
dashboard, just behind the windscreen.
It is also found on a security label
next to the driver's door catch. The
number should agree with those on
the VIL (see below) and in the car's
registration document

VIL sticker
Be sure to note all the numbers on the
Vehicle Identification Label – applied under
the bonnet and also in the service book. This
gives details of the VIN, the colour codes,
model and the options fitted to the car at the
factory (including country code)

Tyres
Be sure to check the
depth across the full wid
the tyre as high pressures
wheel misalignment can c
uneven wear. Also ensure all
are stamped with the app
N-rating and are the same
and speed rating all round

Nose/bonnet
The front end is prone to stone chips. Check and
if repainted, ask where the respray was performed
(to ensure Porsche 10-year paint warranty is intact).
Check under the front bumper for grounding damage
and the headlamp lenses for cracking

Clutch rattle and judder

Listen for a rattle that disappears when you engage the clutch. Be sure to try riding the clutch while the car is on an incline, while reversing or when pulling off slowly. This will test for clutch juddering or slip. Both these symptoms suggest a clutch that may soon need attention

orrosion

Early (pre-2001) 996s can evelop corrosion on the 'B-pillar' nder the door catches. Check for e tell-tale rust blisters

Body Panels

Look along the lines of the car to spot any small dents, imperfections and ripples. Check the underbody, inside the wheel arches, the front compartment and bonnet panel edges and all flexible seals for signs of overspray

Rear Main Seals

Many 996s will suffer from leaking rear main seals (RMS) to a greater or lesser extent. With the car safely raised, check the area between the front of the crankcase and the gearbox for leaks. A light oil film can probably be left until the clutch is changed, but dripping oil will need to be fixed

Wheels/brakes

Carefully check alloy wheels for marks/ chips and signs of poor refurbishment. Ensure they are original Porsche wheels and not after-market copies. Check brake discs for wear (corrosion and blocked holes)

About the authors

Grant Neal

As a long term performance car enthusiast, it was inevitable that my own personal road would lead eventually to Porsche's door. My introduction (back in the late 1980s) was by way of a 250bhp 944 Turbo. The Porsche bug has stayed with me (with a few exceptions) until the present day!

Enthusiastic ownership has allowed me to experience most of the models from the 996 range (over some 6 years) and I am keen to spread the word on these fabulous cars.

Combining the practical knowledge gained from ownership along with in-depth research, I am pleased to be working alongside well known Porsche expert Peter Morgan in presenting this Ultimate Guide to the 996 series 911.

E-mail: grant@sceptre-promotions. freeserve.co.uk

Peter Morgan

Peter Morgan has a Bachelors degree in Mechanical Engineering and trained in the automotive industry. He has written for publication since his teens and became Technical Editor of *Porsche Post* (the magazine of the Porsche Club Great Britain) in 1981. He was Editor from 1991 to 1994. His first Porsche book, *Porsche 911 -- Purchase and DIY Restoration* was published in 1987. To date, he has written 18 titles on all aspects of Porsche, including racing, and his books have been translated into seven languages.

As a professional journalist, he is a member of the Guild of Motoring Writers and contributes to mainstream motoring magazines worldwide.

He offers an independent pre-purchase consultancy for Porsche drivers (www.petermorgan.org.uk)

Acknowledgements

To Porsche AG for certain photos used in the text. Porsche Cars Great Britain, Porsche Cars North America and Porsche Centre Swindon for supplying market-specific data. All other photos: Peter Morgan Media Ltd.

Ultimate Buyers Guides include:

Porsche 911SC 1977 to 1983;
ISBN 0 9545579 0 5
Porsche 911 Carrera 3.2 1983 to 1989
ISBN 0 9545579 1 3
Porsche 944 and 968 (1981-1995)
ISBN 0 9545579 9 9;
Porsche 911 Carrera, Turbo & RS (964)
ISBN 0 9549990 4 5 (2nd Edition)
Porsche 911 Carrera, RS & Turbo (993);
ISBN 0 9549990 1 0 (2nd Edition)
Porsche Boxster & Boxster S 1996 to 2005;
ISBN 0 9549990 0 2 (2nd edition)
Porsche 911 Carrera, Turbo & GT (996)
ISBN 0 9549990 7 X (2nd edition)
MGF and TF
ISBN 0 9545579 6 4
Land Rover Discovery
ISBN 0 9545579 7 2
Subaru Impreza
ISBN 09545579 8 0
Honda Fireblade
ISBN 09549990 4 5 (Mar 07)

And watch out for more new titles!